The 2017 Poetry Marathon Anthology

Edited by

Caitlin Jans

ISBN: 978-1-942344-03-2

Authors Publish Press

Published November 2017

Introduction

Six years ago, my husband, Jacob, and I convinced a few friends and one stranger to write 24 poems in 24 hours at the rate of one poem per hour. We called this event The Poetry Marathon. In the first year there wasn't a half marathon option or pre-made certificates. Only one person, besides Jacob and myself, completed the marathon.

The poems I wrote during that marathon helped me turn http://www.freedomwithwriting.com/freedom/uncategorized/7-publishers-that-pay-150-for-gardening-articles/a corner in my writing. Over half were published. One was nominated for a Pushcart, another selected for a prestigious anthology. Jacob also saw noticeable results, however we would not have pushed forward and hosted other poetry marathons if not for two factors.

The first was encouragement from poets who had attempted the marathon and failed. They read the poems written in the later hours and were impressed by those poems particularly. One poet said she loved "how we all wrote when we got crazy" and she wanted to do a marathon again based on that.

The second was encouragement from poets and friends who had not attempted the marathon at all but had read what we had written. They really wanted us to host a second poetry marathon so they could attempt it. After taking one year off, we hosted a second poetry marathon, and that time over a hundred people signed up. That was the year of the first anthology and the first time the half marathon (12 poems in 12 hours) was an option.

This year was the 5TH Poetry Marathon and this anthology is the third collection of Poetry Marathon poems. Many of the poets in this anthology have participated in three or four marathons or half marathons previously. For some this was their first marathon.

It is important to note that for every year of the marathon I schedule 24 prompts, months before the marathon. The prompts are revealed at the rate of one per hour. The prompts are completely optional but most poets end up using at least one, and some give themselves the additional challenge of following every single one.

Some of the themes that emerge in this anthology come from the prompts, which, in case you were wondering, explains all of the spider poems. Other themes such as exhaustion and insanity emerge more organically.

This year for the first time in the anthology we included the hour each poem was written as well as the geographical location of the poet during the marathon. One of the wonderful aspects of the marathon is the fact that it is so international: poets around the world connect through it.

Still you can see geographic pockets (one in Texas, one in India, one in Washington State) where the marathon has spread through friend groups and family members.

I am very grateful for every person that submitted to this anthology. I am so grateful I got the chance to read your words and that I have the opportunity to share them with others.

Half Marathon

Poems

Colleen Schwartz
Bellingham, Washington, USA
Survivors

You ask: do I write about being a grandmother?
Really, it's too vast.
Like trying to write about
another universe!

This morning, I make note of the honeysuckle blossom,
drifting into the stone birdbath.

Could I possibly write about a boy –
so like his father – and now a big brother?
How would I put words to the scent of
new grandson's head, in that moment
I cradle him at last?

Better to notice these hydrangeas, strong
survivors of summer heat, admired
since our first, small house in Portland.

I thought of children then.

Already lost one.

Dreamed of more.

Shloka Shankar
Bangalore, India
Hour 10

A Tanka

green apples
on a red tablecloth—
how long before
we stop complementing
each other

Hart Crane

Shell-trash and gull-clutter
along the dirty curve
of Revere Beach.
A rough-tongued winter.
The Atlantic churns
its mass of liquid slate
with cold relentlessness.

The sixteen-year-old poet
carries a paperback book
at least twice his age.
A yellowing Oscar
Williams anthology.

He reads the words
of the self-drowned psalmist
of tropic voyages,
Marlovian hymnographer
of azure deeps and steeps.

The sea claimed you,
Hart Crane, as you
claimed the sea, scribe
of brined bones,
of doom and spume,
the merciless ocean's
"bent foam and wave"
swallowing your song.

Liza Kroeschell

San Francisco, California, USA

Hour 8

Just

Now, when he comes home late she just says, "Oh."

Now, when she feels alone she talks to god.

Now, when she suspects the worst she knows it's

Now. Just now. And the coffee tastes wonderful.

Diane Morinich

Norristown, Pennsylvania, USA

Hour 4

Baby Ladies

Baby ladies rule
doing the stroll, doing deeds
unheard of before

Baby ladies primp
and preen
in neon puddles
left by summer storms

Baby ladies blow
pink bubblegum
firecrackers
while luring their prey

Baby ladies climb
into childhood beds with
shredded teddy bears

Baby ladies dream

to be bitches or witches

or women like mom

James Gromis
Berlin, Germany
Hour 6

Untitled

the ragged cliffs
the ever-changing face of mother aqua
the pearls of her tears
caressed by the sunlight

the smoky canyon
blanketed briefly by mist
released to the cold touch
of a young breeze

the uniform fields
of infant barley
slowly raising their crowned heads
to greet the early sun

Cristy Watson
Calgary, Alberta, Canada
Hour 4

Two Thumbs

The coffee shop teems with people –
a ruck of millennials.
Thumbs flying, heads bent;
gaps in the line-up.

Gaps in the line-up –
but nobody cares; they have time.
My coffee break dissipates,
like the mud in my cup.

Thumbs flying, heads bent –
there's a sluggishness to the conversations
once they reach the till; a moment of re-orientation
to the present world.

A ruck of millennials –
I say, 'hang on'; these sophists
will find their way, or the future boasts
babies with two thumbs per hand.

Elisa Shoenberger
Chicago, Illinois, USA
Hour 12

Last Chance

"Last chance to see"
the woman in the scales.
"Come one, come all"
to the Mermaid in a stall.
The man in the checkered suit
waves his gloved hands at the tent.

Last chance to see
a bit of remaining wonder,
a con that only the guileless believed
but we went anyway,
spending our meager cents
for a moment with a woman
who we all pretended to be
more than a woman.

We needed to believe in something
more than the cars on the road,
the orbs of light on the streets,

and the skyscrapers growing into the sky.

We needed a moment that recalled
when humanity lived in fear of the dark,
and knocked on wood to keep the fairies away.
Electricity exposed the outlines of our magic.

We still need the dark.

Jacob Jans

Hour 10

Bellingham, Washington, USA

Forgiveness

I have found a way to forgive the camper's

lit cigarette, the tailgating drivers, the

neighbors who trash their yard and stole apples

from our trees, the bigots who yell

about hell, the poet who judged poems

by the breasts of their authors, the farmer

who stuffs chickens like gas

in the back of his truck, the owners of slot

machines, the teenagers

that beat the crap of out teens; I have

found a way to forgive them all,

and more, to forgive myself, or so

I deceive, knowing ignorance is

so easy these days–

Hafeezah Yates
Ladson, South Carolina, USA
Hour 9

Beloved Spirit

Beloved spirit I know your light is fierce and your flame burns
bright.
I see the turbulence when anxious thoughts cloud your mind in
the middle of the night.
Breathe my love and let wondrous dreams take flight.
Capture the visions of pleasure and indulge as your
subconscious enters into deep delight.
As your body disconnects from the trauma you experienced and
reflects on the most sacred moments in your life.
Beloved spirit let the world miss you as rest overtakes your
precious glow.
Release any inhibitions you held captive during the day and let
spirit flow.
The darkness is your friend and you have permission to engage
in the unseen.
While most people believe this state of being is just a dream.

Lilla Kaszas

Hungary

Hour 6

Impossible

I want to taste it
just one time,
how does it feel
to be loved?

How does it feel
to be loved by someone
for whom you are flawless?

Jeanne Yeasting
Bellingham, Washington, USA
Hour 20 (Second Half Marathon)

Drought

No rain in nearly two months.
The sunshine is glorious, but with no access
to an outdoor spigot or hose, I struggle
to water the garden's plants.

The balcony is long as the house, my mistress's plants plentiful.

She's turned her back.
Again. Walked away;
we're no longer speaking.
The watering can almost empty.

The balcony is long as the house, my mistress's plants plentiful.

NOTE: Poem inspired by: Berthe Morisot, *Young Woman Watering a Shrub,* 1876

Josh Factor

North Carolina, USA

Hour 6

How to travel fearlessly

Just go. Don't even think twice about it.

Turn off your brain and watch yourself sail

Down the highway at top speed come what may.

You may have to come back down every once

In a while to refuel but, once that's done, you're free to soar

Among the heavens once more, not a care in the world,

Waiting for the universe to decide when it's had its fill of you.

Kevin J. O'Conner
Shoreline, Washington, USA
Hour 10

Red

It was a small spot of red
on a canvas dominated by blue and black
a lone point of humanity
amongst two armies
without faces or names

One small spot
to represent the blood
of millions lost

A young woman walked by
stirred by the breeze
the ladybug flew away

Mallika Girotra

Delhi, India

Hour 9

Spider of Depression

Once there was a happy fly,

Roaming here, hopping there,

One day a spider saw her,

Slowly, steadily moving towards the fly,

The spider took her in the grip of her eight legs,

As the first leg tightened, the fly lost concentration,

The second one took her energy,

The third made her aware of her helplessness,

With the fourth leg on her, the fly became hopeless,

Inability to sleep was the fifth gift of the spider to the fly,

She did not want to do the things she liked, and that was the
sixth gift to the fly by the spider,

She became more and more sad about her condition and this
was the gift of the seventh leg of the spider,

As the eighth leg started gripping her, the fly herself wanted to
die,

And hence the spider of depression, fulfilled her last wish by
ending the worst journey of her life.

Not Mine

I felt your hands once, but not as a friend or lover.

I felt your body pressed against mine, in a game of moves
and counter moves.

Silently, secretly… I wanted you to stay there forever.

To embrace you, to feel the warmth and the rightness of you.

I cursed the mocking hands of time as your body left mine,
your comforting presence gone,

reminding me of the void within that I had forgotten so long

ago.

I felt your arms around me once or twice,

feeling slightly more than a cordial farewell embrace.

I closed my eyes and breathed you in, not wanting to say

goodbye.

I *couldn't* tell you that my arms didn't want to let you go,

I *couldn't* tell you that my heart hoped you didn't want to let

go of me, too.

So I smiled and laughed, a carefully constructed mask put in place.

You could see me, but not the tearing of what I felt underneath.

The need to protect you was a compelling force, so a facade went up,

and every handkerchief of interest I could drop stayed within my pockets.

I think of you every day, though I shouldn't.

Nothing inappropriate or improper, but even so…

You are not mine, so I cannot be yours.

Not even in my dreams.

The truth of that ringing the bluest of tunes through the hollows of my soul.

Though love does not truly hold your heart,

     I do not wish it to ever be broken.

Stand tall and strong, man of the earth, for you are.

You are like the Oak tree who has learned to bend like the Willow.

What draws me to you, if not this kind of strength?

I do not know if you see me from afar, or if you even think of me -

the way I think of you.

Selfishly, I could hope for that.

But I am *not* selfish, nor can I make you see me if you do not already.

I do not have a halo of light surrounding me,

nor an air of superficiality pouring from my being -

marking me as a creature of perfection.

Just because I yearn for you – though I can never tell you that truth –

doesn't mean I'm the kind of woman you would ever yearn for in return.

Yet, underneath my moral code, I wish I were.

These feelings are irrational and illogical, I know.

I do not know you or your depths, nor do you know me or mine.

And yet I wish… I wish I could know you and all the secrets you hide.

I would guard them with my heart and with my life.

I wish you could know me and the abyss of secrets I hold,

but only if you would guard *me* with your heart and your life.

I wish we could discover what could've been,

if time and circumstance had been on my side.

Insanely, impossibly, I feel as though you are my missing
piece.

No… it is not a delusion, nor am I insane. I feel the impossible
truth of it.
Somehow, you could complete the puzzle that is me.
If you should ever find yourself free, think of me.
If you were mine, I could be yours.
Together, we could discover the worlds that lay at our feet,
and we would know an all consuming love,

    that not even eternity could quench.

Brian Sluga
Houston, Texas, USA

My First Marathon

It was 1980 something and the gun shoots
runners off
one step two step
running with the stride like no other
it passes quickly the 10k mark
my mind is daft
my body chaffed and burnt
at 13 miles, I get a second wind
I am indulging in what I do
fatigue is not an option
20th mile I'm sore and wrecked
with my conscience, I endure
question myself and wonder why I am here
remember the miles, sweat and blisters
finally, I can see the crowds and finish
I cross the line and collapse
a journey of endless proportions
in a few hours, I'm planning another
the addition has started

twenty-six miles 365 yards

that's me sorted

my time here is done

Laurel Wilson

Mammoth, Arizona, USA

Hour 9

Black Widow Teaches

Out here in the desert,
Everybody bites, pinches, or stings.

When my hound learned rattlesnakes were bad
(I was grateful for the fence between them)
My neighbor taught me to
Pin its head and neck with something heavy
Decapitate it with a shovel (don't touch it because it can still
Bite) and drop it in the septic access pipe.

The hound was so proud of himself he
Bayed at the garden hose for half an hour.

I use a snake stick now if they're too close to the house, and
Release those rattlers in their range.
I was a girl with a
Toad in a jar or a jar full of flies for my
Lizards or a wild snake in my grubby hands,
Gently returning him home after a some probably

Terrifying gigantic admiration.

We've got scorpions, sun spiders, gila monsters, coral snakes,
Fire ants, kissing bugs, raccoons, coyote, and
Cougar (she was using the treehouse as a
Feeding perch and it took a pitched pile of rocks before she
picked a better
Restaurant).

An honored guest
Tarantula lives in my basement and eats
Cockroaches.

So a black widow in the door jamb
Near the carport
Really didn't bother at all. I said
Hi to her as I came and went to work.

But the mutual non-aggression policy
Failed when I saw that sack of eggs.

Bleach in a bottle was in easy reach, so I
Squirted it on the cocoon of her lives.

I figured, I figured...

It doesn't matter what I figured because

Black Widow Mother sprinted to her eggs. She

Leapt back as she approached the stink. She knew it was

Poison; she walked a jittery circle away and back twice.

I figured, I figured...

It doesn't matter what I figured because her

Frantic legs straddled drops of death clinging to her guy wires

and she

Plucked up that sodden silk purse of destroyed hope;

Away she went, wobbling, slowing, absorbing toxic

extermination

So she could save her babies.

Aghast, I watched her die, her body in death still

Clutching the corpse cocoon.

I figured, I figured...

It doesn't matter what I figured because

I was wrong.

Julia Mikus
Columbus, Georgia, USA
Hour 4

The Waters Call

The waters call to him,
no matter where he goes.
He longs for the beauty,
the waters gentle flow.
The waters call to him,
the love his sons do share.
They spend time on the water,
laughing without care.
The waters call to him,
lake, stream, and ocean wave.
He finds healing in the sound.
The rest his soul does crave.
The waters call to him,
no matter where he roams.
The waters call to him,
for there he finds his home.

Hannah Nguyen
Seattle, Washington, USA

The Reaper Visits a Celebrating Town

Gray clouds precede the midnight black
once arrived, coats the sky in ink –
magenta sparks explode in the air,
followed by gold, crimson, emerald, and sapphire –
on the roof, a man lights another firework.
The rocket blooms in the sky,
casting a kaleidoscope of multicolored smoke on
slate stone buildings border the streets –
connected awning to awning by tawny ropes
hanging lanterns cast citrine glows below –
where crowds shuffle between chestnut walls
and mahogany planks of run-down buildings.
Nearby, in a darkened alleyway,
the silver sword escapes its sheath.
White strips of bandage unravel around the blade
revealing rows of runes glowing azure blue
in the air slowly darkening with dusk.
A hooded stranger folded in ragged cloaks of black
spins and plunges the sword –

in the dimness, a body falls –

staining the cobblestones with scarlet.

Jayne Marek

Port Townsend, Washington, USA

Hour 5

The Low Ride (Thirteeners)

As water slides around a stone, borrowing its shape,

our black-and-white cat Sylvester, long and rangy, walks

near our legs but doesn't want a pat, so suddenly

as he passes, and we lean over with one hand out,

he dips beneath it, somehow: from his withers to hips

he continues traveling but flows under and up

to return to his original horizontal.

Flexible, mysterious, even magical, he

chooses to be close yet keep his distance. Cat as cat.

Jessica Swafford

Lexington, Kentucky, USA

Hour 8

The Closest

One Christmas

I gave you a Zippo lighter

with the ace of spades

engraved upon its metal case.

It was custom ordered,

a connection to your dead daddy.

After unwrapping your gift,

your hands and voice were shaky.

That was the closest

I ever came

to seeing you cry.

Michele K. Smith

Birdsboro, Pennsylvania, USA

Hour 5

Time Capsule (a Rondeau)

This time capsule in my mind's tomb
I step inside my past, and loom
grounded by olive patchwork floor
always slightly off-kilter door
memories of my girlhood room

Do glow-in-the-dark stars illume
the ceiling still? Can I presume
a child pretends there once more
this time capsule in my mind's tomb

Antique mirror to primp, dare, groom
behold the wild flower bloom
Paneled walls too thin to ignore
the chaos of those days of yore
Will I return? I don't assume
this time capsule in my mind's tomb

C.K. Nickell

Fort Worth, Texas, USA

Hour 11

Freedom

Floating off on the sea, pulled out by the tide.

Starting a new adventure with the stars as my guide.

The only sound is the water flowing past the hull.

There is no need for light for the moon is bright and full.

I am on this journey alone, but I am not afraid.

I laid out a plan, and bowed my head and prayed.

The wind lifts my hair and cools the salt on my skin.

Happiness overcomes me, and I cannot help but grin.

I am free of the chains that held me for so long.

I am ready to write my own story and sing my own song.

Black Widow

Hey big boy...
Wanna have some fun?

I may eat you.
But maybe I won't.

Like goin' out on a limb?
You're not chicken are you?

Come home to mamma.
Hit a home run.

Find out about my name
if you've got the nerve.

Maybe we'll just hang.
Catch a few flies.

You could bring a computer,

spend some time on the web.

Life's no fun without risk.

You could talk to my last sweetie
but he's out of town for a while.

Don't hang like a sloth.

Come on over,
I've got some stories to spin.

Joy Winstead

Mogador, Ohio, USA

Hour 8

Let Me Tell You

As a writer, I'll

write and tell

me and you

all about how

I'm laying in the

sun and in the sun

lay a dying rose.

After Emily Dickinson's A Day

Aymen Zaheer
Lahore, Pakistan
Hour 2

Yearning for Spring

love rules me and my heart

which you captured at the start

the day we met the bounteous day

fate will and my yearning to obey

an awesome lesson on silent face

that added wonder and some grace

it conjured within me a new life

while pouring the love in hive

the way you said; I love you dear

i peep into words, not merely hear

the movement, they engrossed in me

pains turn to fragrance, spread and free

standing aloof, once I thought

what was I, where I have been brought?

something radiates me with soundless word

i love you too, you flower, am a bird

in the late April, I strongly felt

meet my spring and make it melt

Not Today

'Think of a team name,' you say,
'We'll be inseparable from that day.
I want us to be as tight as a rope,
I want you to be my handler,
My friend and my hope,
I'm barely using these days –
Practically clean,
And I love you bumhead.'
That's what you said.

'Think of a team name,' you say,
But what's the point?
We both know it will always escape your memory
But never your lips
That it'll just be a forgotten memory
From one of your trips,
And you'll roll a joint
Just to take the edge off...
And forget what you said.

'Think of a team name,' you say,

And I want to do the whole thing –

Team colours to wear and a team song to sing,

A motto, a mascot,

But you do this a lot –

Get me to dream

By mentioning things you only temporarily mean.

I wait for the comedown to start

And brace my still-high heart.

'Think of a team name,' you say,

And I don't want to –

Not today.

C H Bailey
Mebane, North Carolina, USA

Hour 9

Volta

We looked so carefree and happy, and
no one was allowed to know that we were not.
We maintained the requisite image — laughing and waving.
No one saved us from the black waters underneath; but
we saved ourselves. And we are no longer drowning.

After Stevie Smith's poem, "Not Waving But Drowning"

Rainbows

A sliver of light

peeking behind darkness.

A giggle

heard somewhere in between wails.

There is always something

in the midst of nothingness.

Like the north star

in a sea of lights,

find that one small thing

to be your constant companion.

Joy.

Let me choose joy over this barrage of misery.

After all rainbows come after the rain.

Qundeel Aymen
Lahore, Pakistan
Hour 11

Dream

In the streams of stars

I expect your hand

Where we walk and dance

On the imaginary island

The beeps of birds

The silence of love

And the whispering of water

All are fading from my world

Mary-Jeanne Smith
Dayton, Washington, USA
Hour 11

A Perfect Moment

Adventurer don't wallow, break through the glorious morn.
Dance, twirl, about with joy, don't stop the breath from
breathing.

The heart breaks no longer, the time has come for boundaries
safe.
All around is heavenly laughter, bubbling over brooks of glee.

Time stands still upon this mountain, with flower filled fields of
contentment.
Life is, momentarily, complete.

Ricard Enos

Houston, Texas, USA

8 Hour

Nimru the Shadow Thief

Beware simple merchant traveling with rich wares

His price is always right but the cost ensnares

Delicious sweets, gold or bountiful seed

All with foul taint to make a soul bleed

Your neighbors covet and cannot stay away

Everyone withers and falls into dismay

Their shadows scream and twist into nil

Bent fast to the Shadow Thief's will

The day after greenish horrid things rise

In the night listen for their sorrowful cries

The Shadowless wander forever bound

Seeking lost shadows never to be found

Joan Leotta

Calabash, North Carolina, USA

Hour 11

Swallowtail Jig

Dancing from bloom to bloom,

swallowtail offers her

yellow and black wings

as contrast to the bright

blue of cloudless sky

and roadside's array of

purple Mexican petunias.

She flits from bloom to bloom,

tapping her delicate toes

into pollen—some for her,

some for the next plant

on her stage.

Morgan Taylor

Fort Collins, Colorado, USA

Hour 11

An Elegiac Sonnet For Wilfred Owen

Eleven months, eleven days, and where

were you when they began to ring the bells

to tell the world that everything you had

fought with such horror for, was done again?

They'd stilled the demon war once more and there

was shouting in the streets and toffs and swells

who'd read your words, and thought them sad,

put them aside to take out now and then.

Do you suppose they knew just where you'd gone?

That words were all they'd ever know of you?

Or were they lost in dreams of hope and glory,

not caring who had paid, and was withdrawn?

I read your words and know it's never true.

Dulce's never been pro patria mori.

Kathleen J Kidder
Nashville, Tennessee, USA
Hour 7

Terror Inside

I hear the chilling sound of his voice
as I recognize behind me
the cold click-clack of the shotgun loading.

Barely able to breathe, I lift my eyes from
the plates in my hands to
see his reflection, in the
window over the sink. I see his evil smirk.

"Are you ready to finish that fight now?"
My heart racing, electricity
surging through my body, in slow
motion, I turn to face him.

Fear so intense I lose
control of my body; seeing me
standing in my own puddle, he
laughs and walks out again.

Humiliated and terrified, I
drop to the floor and

weep for my babies, praying

they will never know this terror.

Charlotte Barna

Carmichael, California, USA

Hour 7

Guts

Let's start with the organs and tissue and bone for once,

Instead of mountainous breasts and slender legs.

If we really really looked into the eyes,

Rather than just noting the shocking blue

That makes her so pretty,

We'd see so much more.

Look into them and see her suffering,

Because if you understand her suffering you understand her.

His muscles are bulging beneath his tank top,

But what if you saw the actual biceps underneath.

Then you could see the real struggle,

The pounds of pain he lifts up and away,

The pain that keeps coming back.

Maybe that's why he is so huge.

Feel the heart, transporting blood,

Instead of thinking you know the heart,

Based on a few misspoken words.

Words are hard, cut them some slack.

Bones are strength.

Bent over a walker, she is not weak.

Her bones have been through more than you could fathom,

Her back just needs a permanent rest,

From every thing she's supported all her years.

Karol Cyrklaff

Sacramento, California, USA

Hour 11

The party had just begun

Relativistic perpetuation

running rampant

engulfing the turf

Portending catastrophe,

there is a loud crack,

booming from behind

The water cascades in,

cacophony complete

a thunderous rumbling underneath

From the wall's collapse,

there is no return.

Run

There is nothing left

behind

ahead is full of dread.

Bound on,

adrenal excitement

boiling over into reality.

William Jackson
Saratoga Springs, Utah, USA
Hour 9

Spider Apprentice

May I apprentice to—
master spider beings;
specialized in floating thread,
alight on gentle breeze.
Keeping secret—webcraft,
tying dreams to heaven,
turning death to hopefulness,
by perfect artistry.

John Cryar

Conroe, Texas, USA

Hour 4

A Friend In Need

Like rain drops falling from the sky,

they appear at my house.

I've looked at my door,

to see if there is some special mark,

like the hobos of old made

for friendly stops.

Of course, I find none, knew I wouldn't.

They know just the same.

A friend in times of need lives here.

Some are just passing through,

others, too sick or too tired, stay.

With that special vision they have,

cats know where a friend lives.

Those that stay I rename with

What they reveal to me.

I give them all the same middle name – Lucky.

All their needs are met, by me and by the vet.

I provide unconditional love and peace,

and the vet, she does her thing too.

Sometimes they linger and grow healthy,

other times they just linger for the hospice.

Either way, I love them all,

and they respond in kind.

J. Pratt-Walter

Vancouver, Washington, USA

Hour 5

INFP

For the introvert, the harvest
of spoken syllables is
meager.
Go on, ask a friend
for her spare
words. Ask your husband;
he doesn't know how to be
quiet.
Ask yourself "Is this garden really
worth it?"
I assure you, it is. Dig down.
Friends and husbands are fine,
but your garden of thoughts can feed
the hungering world.

Jo Eckler

Austin, Texas, USA

Hour 1

Relief

The moment when,

mud-crusted, bog-heavy, sun-singed,

the breeze lifts your chin,

tilting your face to meet

the first drop.

Street Performers

A usual day it was.
The streets were busy,
People were doing their things
All of a sudden, out of nowhere,
came a little girl in orange frock,
and a man of about forty.
He had a violin.
They came running,
and started performing.
The man played and girl broke into a jig,
With her hair moving with

her,
legs.
tapping my hands.
them,
too,
together, holding hands,
audience became artists.
I'm in until very long,
to think.
one,
between.
went,

Dancing with the rhythm of her
I couldn't stop myself from
Somebody joined
and somebody else
Three of them jigged
One by one, the
I never realized
There was nothing
They waited for no
There were no pauses in
They came, danced and then
and left our hearts jigging.

74

That day, all my way back home,

I was humming, shaking and smiling,

smiling at nothing.

They remind me of the long lost reunions.

They woke the vibrant girl up.

Zara Thomson
Regina, Saskatchewan, Canada
Hour 7

Inside Out

Inside

A heartbeat bold and brave

willing to serve or fight

blood infused with high standards

a thoughtful mind

strong bones to endure

reserved lips

generous teeth

observing eyes

sympathetic ears to listen

hands to lift and hold

humble knees

onward moving feet

a face, the welcome sign

presents a person from the

Outside

Empress

"She's not allowed in the bedroom,"
I said
When we brought our kitten home.

She cried outside our door, and
I relented.
"She can come in during the day."

She slept curled up behind my knees.
I loved it.
The cat, she ruled our house.

She snacked on aloe and creeping Charlie.
I wanted plants.
"We'll put them high on the shelf."

She liked to drink from toilet bowls.
I disapproved.
We flushed, and left lids raised.

She plotted to watch birds out of windows.

I cleared the sills.

The cat, she ruled our house.

She pushed her food onto the floor.

I hated the mess.

We bought deeper bowls, and floor mats.

She deposited hair on clothes and blankets.

I winced, shook my head.

We learned to love the lint brush.

She followed me with dogged intent.

I carried her. Always.

This cat, she ruled my heart.

Catarina Marron

Desert Hot Springs, California, USA

Hour 1

Heart and Soul

She lived alone

The loneliness stayed

surrounded by many everyday

In a heart and soul made

a California Girl

too country for this world

Longing for the right love

in the right place and time

Inside lies the darkness of life displayed

The smile she stays

shown on her face each day

The heart hurt with pain

shadows of a life in vain

A simple life she cries for

A front porch swing she longs for

An old school country girl

drowning in this out of place of this world

drove off to Tennessee today…..

Angel of Flight

My Favorite Color, Midnight Blue

Often times,

when I lie on my bed at night,

I imagine what my ideal room would be like.

The first thought that comes to mind

is what color the walls would be.

For me, there's only one solid answer –

midnight blue.

The best part is that

midnight blue is the color of the sky at night,

so that whenever I would lie on my bed,

it'd feel like I'm outside looking up the stars.

I could have that majestic feeling

wash over all the time

with the color midnight blue

all over my walls.

That feeling that all my dreams could come true,

and that, by far, is the best feeling to have.

Coming back to reality,

I look wistfully at the purple walls of bedroom.

Purple is probably my third or fourth favorite color,

but it's not the best color for a room.

Instead, midnight blue is and always will be that color for me.

Inside Out

Looking from the inside out,
casts a spell of vociferous self-doubt…
I wear a black cloak, a mage's hat,
say abracadabra, have a black cat.

But no sorcery will make my demons disappear,
I feel their dogged shadows foraging near…
I wave my wand, drink an obviating potion.
Inside out is too bare, a revealing notion.

I hide my face of Veritas, don a vacant mask,
keeping inside in is a rather insidious task…
Don't let Them see, don't let Them know –
so much of me I just dare not show

So much that's fragile and reticent,
I'm complicated, elusive and omnipotent…
There's an abyss within me which I must never expose,
best keep it concealed, best nobody knows.

Looking from the outside in,

blemished heart bleeds tainted sin…

Can you love me, think you truly can?

Even being so damned inside out that I am?

Mus(e)ic

Long blonde hair, bound by a band,
pleated pants and dressy polyester blends.
Holding sheet music in one hand,
and that drink she recommends.
Setting up as the crowd murmurs
sweating, shifting, settling in his seat.
Silence yields from his observers,
but he's trembling for a beat.
Ivory and black blurs betwixt his palms,
until he sees a glimpse of her,
gallantly glimmering, she calms
him from afar, drinking her coffee liqueur,
she listens as he lulls, forgotten the fear
from prior to her being near.

Heidi Garnett

Kelowna, British Columbia, Canada

Hour 5

Nowy Dwor Gdanski Once Known as Home

The scythed hay in the field has dried

and an old woman now rakes it into piles.

She smiles and waves as I stop to catch my breath

beneath an ancient linden tree, its split trunk

held together with wire mesh,

mesh grown to wood, wood grown to flesh,

flesh grown to bone, this struggle to stand upright,

to remember the sun's warmth on your back

as you fled through the snow. I wonder

does the sun rise out of habit each morning

or because it knows a day without hope is unbearable?

Tasselled blossoms dangle from pale yellow bracts,

their perfume the scent of honey stirred in tea,

the scent of home.

Bee trees my mother called them.

Jane Rittenhouse
Eugene, Oregon, USA

The Jig

Dance a jig upon the ridge

with foaming surf below

to whisk and blend with sky and wind

and spirit, to and fro.

Quickly as the bow reveals

the tones and tunes array

the Celtic lines, do re-define

the balance, and the fray.

Fiddle quick and fiddle fine

Bestir an ancient fire

Music as a tinderbox

creation to inspire.

Sue Storts
Tulsa, Oklahoma, USA
Hour 3

Ekphrastic Selfie Poem

The light is just right.

Background of red and beige,

embellished with dark brown dots.

Creases ironed in muslin,

crow's feet

if crows had eighteen toes.

Alien furrows

between brown caterpillars,

over a drooping but decorated squint.

Folds like elephant skin

spread around the smile,

seersucker button below.

A pillar of crepe draperies

falls in folds for support.

Spots and crevices that

don't show in the mirror.

Sunlight reveals

the scene it helped create.

Yearning

At five, "A shepherdess" I answered,
imagining the tender lamb of a bedtime poem,
open freedom of the meadows and valleys, and
a gentle pace of active, outside work.

At fifteen, "An actress" I replied
for the thrill of self-discovery and performance,
my commanding voice carrying to the back wall
where I would connect with last row's quiet spectators.

"A world traveler" with confident dreams at twenty-five
I had journeyed half a world away,
falling in love with the people of castles,
fountains, knights, windmills, and castanets.

As my brother grew sick, I again found the beauty of home,
revisiting our memories in bus rides,
childhood swings, and climbed trees
before the final goodbye.

At thirty-five I knew the desire of wanting

Time to stop. Time to grow. Time to learn. Time to teach.
Time to discover, laugh, dream, bicker, cry, giggle, and share
deepest delight just once more.

At forty-five, I prayed for "grace and peace"
in tender moments of quietly sitting, holding hands, sighing
memories,
humming songs, and thanking first my father then my best friend
for our times together, the blessings they had been.

Now at fifty, a shepherdess' steadfast protection over gentle ones
appeals to me.
Teaching for a lifetime, can my voice carry to that student in the last
row?
Spanish coasts and mountains beckon me to a pilgrimage as if I
were young again.
Yearning for adventures of the spirit, this time I carry those I'll
forever love.

Samantha Hagan

Tallahassee, Florida, USA

Hour 6

8 Legged Freak

Dear Mr. or Mrs. Spider,

Keep to your side of the shower

take out the:

mosquitos

gnats

flies

other spiders who won't sign this agreement

keep to your side of the shower

we'll get along just fine

if it has more legs than I do

have at them, hide the bodies when you're done

I don't want to know what you get up to

keep to your side of the shower

we'll get along just fine

I promise to leave your web alone where

I see those eight shiny black eyes watching (why do you have

one for each leg?!)

keep to your side of the shower

we'll get along just fine

Virginia Carraway Stark

Dawson Creek, British Columbia, Canada

Hour 2

Emerald Cut

The pool was made of turquoise wind

the edges sculpted

an emerald cut tapered up

of perfect teal

Hidden in its high setting

protective mountains

coated in diamond dust

glaciers

that dripped

merciless cold

from the dawn of time

with endless purity

into the vast jewel

leaping high with strange inclusions

jumping fish

living waters

pouring out into the evermore

Sheila Sondik
Bellingham, Washington, USA
Hour 9

(tanka)

fat orb weaver
squatting in her web
centrally located
a soft plucking at the edge
announces a tiny doomed suitor

Muse

Some say that inspiration

is the work of muses in our heads.

My muse is stubborn, obnoxious, dull.

He throws about the papers

in the office of my brain.

"Give me inspiration!" I demand.

He laughs and takes a nap.

I can't be expected to do his job!

Look at how he's wrecked them,

all my good ideas.

Now, never-finished stories sit

(I suspect he ate the ends).

When I put a pen to paper,

my muse becomes quite riled.

He snatches everything I might have used

and hides away in some deep cavern.

I think he must be minuscule

to do damage so tremendous.

His hair is long and blue and spiky,

And his eyes a scheming green.

I asked for beauty, emerald forests,

Instead, he gives me this.

Does his ego know no bounds!?

When will his antics cease!?

Well…

I guess the poem wasn't bad…

But he still won't get a raise!

Maria Riofrio

New York, New York, USA

Hour 3

Let there be Light

I wish I could emanate light

in one, long, straight shot to the world

to say I am here, I am alive,

I am ok.

But a long time ago I lost that light;

Illumination was taken from me

when I could not defend myself.

And whatever spark remained has kept me

just bright enough to get by,

to avoid the dark obstacles of human interaction,

but not yet to shine.

Ruchi Chopra

Brecksville, Ohio, USA

Hour 3

Bennu

she soaked her dreams, yearnings, anxieties,
and hunger in the aroma of mulberry paper; her favorite
among other aromas – spicy, torrid, arid, humid
and provocative.

Her unbounded spirit and hunger
savor cactuses, orchids, and ambrosia –
between mythical pauses: her spiritual cauldron
persists against dominance – a mix tape of dissonance and
resonance.
{cultural mitosis} {transgressions}

provoked from centuries after centuries – she is 'reborn.'
as a Bennu – a bird
with a voracious hunger
from which sprouts thousands of fireflies.

like a suckling seedling she breathes
in sprigs, herbs, bones, carcasses,

cactus thorns, poison ivies, and tumbleweeds.

{leftovers} Karmic deeds

Nirvana {cigarette smoke rings}

Janel Davis

Bellingham, Washington, USA

Hour 5

The Bereaved

Smoke has crept over her, and then to the city,
so I can't see the ocean from my home anymore.

The B.C. trees have gone up in flame and now
go down to the water to drink salty waves.

They can't quench anything, but
smother the salt scent.

The white wave foam catches the edge of smoke,
pulling it over her briny body like a shroud.

And we, the bereaved, stand watch—
claiming each then to wait for her own.

Naida Nepascua-Supnet
Pasig City, Philippines
Hour 7

From Someone who is Shy

Hey guys listen up from someone who is shy
from her meek little smiles to her words that say why
underestimate not what this shy one can do
she can move every mountain and might defeat you

hey guys listen up from someone so secretive
from someone whom we thought was never active
belittle her never for she might overpower
all those that are loud and those that clatter

hey you all of you who are so unbeatable
quiet ones are deadly lethal and able
they can mesmerize crowds when they start to speak
we'll find out they are strong and was never been weak

for quiet ones are thinkers and analytical
waiting for a moment a chance and a call
and when they begin to speak all their minds
we'll be blown and in awe for the true masterminds.

John S Green

Bellingham, Washington, USA

Hour 11

Farmers Market Sounds

The buzz of the local farmers market resonates closer with
every step,

music and singing tickle my ears.

Young girls on ukuleles, a string-band stomping in ballad,

street performers juggling—delighting the young families

slurping up ice cream,

toasted cinnamon almonds, Bavarian pretzels.

Fresh scents of basil, dill, cilantro, lavender float around the
square…

and tomatoes, melons, potatoes, zucchini, squash, cucumbers
abound.

I stand still, eyes closed, letting a fiddle take me away.

Caroline Jupp
London, UK
Hour 7

Faintly the Frigate

There must be something
something I can say
to get us out of this
as bad as it is foolish
that fight on the roof of the train
dangling by a finger
and a thumb in your eye.

Perhaps out of shot actors
who roam the foreshore
can dramatize our scene
discuss motivations
for a redundant queen
to promote a goodwill claim
and figure this migrating ship.

Megha Punjabi
Lucknow, India
Hour 3

My Solace

My solace
is where I hear no cry;
And when my heart
speaks to the mind.

For, things done
and the things undone!
The heart, which is barren
and lost all hope.

You can start afresh,
says the mind.
This time, do as you fancy
For you can please none, but yourself!

Britton Gildersleeve
Blacksburg, Virginia, USA
Hour 2

She is writing her self-portrait

rolling words within her mouth
like the finely pointed tip of a brush
its camel bristles viridian green
While the broader brush beside it
glistens with a simpler blue
simple as mountain air is simple
blue with the evening damp
a thin mist of blue and grey
and the promise of evening rain
Not simple at all, really

The lines she hopes will sing
quiver like the strings
of the untuned harp in the corner
that still holds the memory
of music within tensile wires
hum in sympathy to colours and textures
palette knife and finger
stone and rag and bone
she knows she must include

How will she draw the rivers

she wonders

the earthy Mekong brown

the silverine of the Chao Phraya

the red clay of the Arkansas

the chatoyance of this newest friend

For now, she is an island

in a confluence of waters

how their currents fed her from wide beds

how she moved over and through

their slick finned stories

It is more than hesitating brush and ink

are able in her faltering hand

to render

the cacophony that masquerades

as her name, her face

how it changes colours

as the rivers widen shorten deepen

each a note on a staff in a lyric

that needs more music to move

as the wind does   as the birds do

as she did each year of her fragmented childhood

in arcs of bright morning light

in swooping loops of flight

in the scalloped surfaces of rivers

that might as well be her own blood

circling in pulsing rhythm

her faceless homeless heart

Katie Dunne
Chicago, Illinois, USA
Hour 1

Orion

watch

me

catch

stars

before

they

fade

Michelle Banner

Philadelphia, Pennsylvania, USA

Hour 1

Second chances

Fresh like the morning dew

Clear and concise uncommonly nice. Motivation in over drive regrets covered in broken promises have no power today.

Today my opportunity to fly is bigger than my fear

No longer will my voice fall on deaf ears

Today the world will know

I was here

Nicole Harlow

Canoga Park, California, USA

Hour 8

The Ring's Temptation

she will forgive

her temptations of these

her thoughts of wild

her dreams and –

dreams of power wandering

in the forest, the throes of cries

images of confusions

in the pools of

the waters; a

power that subsides, wasted

what is old, now her youth

Gracelynn Lau

Shawnigan Lake, British Columbia, Canada

Hour 6

A healer's memo to self

can we do it differently this time?

you sheltered my confusion

in your darkness, mistakenly

I thought the lunar eclipse

was a proven good omen

for our divine arrangement

how careless I was

to have not noticed

my oceanic plate

was subducted under

your continental margin

can we do it differently this time?

you risked everything to treasure hunt

an answer you had lost

half a century ago

I thought the signs were plentiful

enough for you to leap

over the fringe to the other side

that you've always wanted to belong

how childish I was

to have not seen

your unwillingness to start anew

that your warrior hunt

was just another exotic vacation

can we do it differently this time?

you landed inside the barricade

of my conscious awareness

with sophisticated conclusions

so honorable that deserves

extra generous handling

I thought the unseen was at work

in the orchestral timing for us

to venture into the undiscovered interior landscape

how inattentive I was

to have missed your clues

that the medicine at hand

is not ready to be consumed

Molly Hickok

Lemon Grove, California, USA

Hour 7

The Beginning is the End

If I bring you the whole bush

It'll be a chill time

But I know better now

I hope you like these flowers

Words are fun to write

Here is where it starts

Words are out of sight

Picking them took hours

I'll bring you the whole bush somehow.

Just another way to kill time.

The flowers won't die or smush.

Tanya LaForce
Muncie, Indiana, USA
Hour 11

That Swallowtail Jig

there is a calling, they say
all the night things must comply
the music of all shall fill the night
a splendid sound it shall be
a story; right of passage, if you will
a joyous, jubilant journey
which must be fulfilled
this is the way of the night
an old sacred right, not to be ignored
the rhythm pours out in waves
the journey of the calling becomes complete
as the music and the night things become one

Richard Osler

Duncan, British Columbia, Canada

Hour 10

Walking Back to the House

I want a colour with wilderness inside it.

A colour untouched without ashes in it.

I was given a colour of smoke once. I ate it.

I was given a pewter bell and told to ring it.

I rang it so long it bled silver gray

on the rope in my hand.

I want a colour with forgiveness in it.

A colour, sage green, I can crush in my hand.

After, I want to smell hope and possibility.

I was held hostage by a colour wearing a black balaclava.

I refused to kneel and close my eyes.

That colour stunk of absence and rage.

It wasn't a stranger. This was the day

I became colour blind.

Aaron Silverberg

Bellingham, Washington, USA

Hour 3

Colorscape

lapis lazuli is the color of my spiritual doorway.

tourmaline, the color of our marriage stones.

fingertip berry is the color of satiation.

our guacamole house sports both

avocado yellow and green.

honey – the highlight color of doors, deck

and cedar shake.

silver/green lichen,

at the base of massive cedars,

is the color of patience.

when cedar is exploded by lightning

or thrashed to the ground by winter wind,

its orange-red flesh disintegrates

into miniature Medieval towns.

after many months it breaks down

into a soft duff I love to walk through
barefoot.

when my feet are well stained orange-red,
I am ready to join the moist and thoughtful sanctuary.

Natasha Vanover
North Miami Beach, Florida, USA
Hour 12

My Mother's Clothes

Sporty...

Chic... cotton, silk, and linen.

She prefers Indian cotton, like how she dresses her babies.

Clothes that move; clothes that breathe.

She is Grace personified, on-trend, and a classic who
dresses for herself.

She is on trend because she is a classic who dresses for herself.

She was "athleisure" before it was in vogue.

She wears pastels, whites, and royal blues with such command.

Denim shorts and gingham tops are how she shops.

My mother is a pillar of fashion and fun.

I feel her radiance, her energy, as powerful as the sun.

Hollywood Swimming Pool

From my perspective,

headless socialites don't need to learn how to swim,

they are buoyed up by their falsies.

At 3 feet, the greatest social trauma seems to be the lack of a

Brazilian.

For those who have gone off the deep end,

there is a ghost from a 70's party

doing that dance move with the pointy finger

up and down.

At 12 feet, I find ditched wedding rings,

multicolored teaser condoms,

a lone martini glass rolling across the bottom.

Everyone remains pretty shallow,

by comparison,

the deep end is not for sissies.

Sublime Epic

There were hedgehogs
(Imagine hedgehogs)

There were nuns
(Imagine nuns)

On the same woodland path
(One after the other)

Paul Sarvasy

Bellingham, Washington, USA

Hour 2

Travel Card

In my wallet, I still keep
the travel card you gave me in 1973
which grants the bearer, me,
immediate and instant passage to somewhere else.

This 2 by 3 inch rounded edge card stock,
illuminated in black ink
from a 00 rapidograph pen,
I hold for an emergency.

The front side shows your
drawings of our first months together,
while the back lists
those places of desire.

Over the years, the edges have
curled and frayed leaving
some of the journey locales

and memories in doubt.

It was from a time
when it was just the three of us,
you, me, and Peter the cat,
with your dragon blowing hot air onto our bed.

My card numbered 0000001 does not give
instructions in how I can use it.
Do I need to hold it, click my heels
three times, and think of where I want to go?

I have never asked you
if you have card number 0000002,
if the same destinations are on it,
and if you have used it.

Alena Casey
California, USA
Hour 12

What We Were

He was a sun who wanted a moon.
I was the snowflake that melted at noon.

He was a house who wanted a home.
I was the bird that needed to roam.

He was a clerk who wanted a number.
I was the word that warned of his blunder.

He was a lover who wanted a tryst.
I was the wind that could never be kissed.

He was a man who wanted me
And everything I could not be.

Bia Riaz
Sacramento, California, USA
Hour 17 (Second Half Marathon)

Earth Gazing

Hello little blue planet
I'm worried about you
I've been watching you
You don't look so well
Did you stop taking care of yourself?

Nestled in your celestial sky
I've seen your past, present, and future
I've seen your shiny whites and brilliant blues
Luscious greens and amber golds
Swirling and sliding, shifting and changing.

Lately, your kaleidoscope is murky
Dark, dull, foreboding spots and patches
Damaged and ruined
I'm worried you won't be able to breathe

Maybe you should stop smoking.

Full Marathon

Poems

Space Dog

Not given a choice
a homeless pet,
captured and kept
her fate had been set.

A kiss on her nose
a final farewell,
one night as a pet
a normal day met.

What could she do?
a sacrifice yet,
for science she went
to the stars she'd been sent.

What were her thoughts?
her fear had been great,
she couldn't guess when
her life would end then.

Janice Raquela Mendonca

Mumbai, India

Hour 7

A Newborn's First Thoughts

Where am I?

And how did I get here?

Hang on.... this... place smells funny...

Why is everything so bright?

Why am I surrounded by all these men in strange caps and

surgical gloves?

Who are these giants?

Did that doctor just whack my bum?

Ouch! Watch it!

Does anyone here speak baby?

Where are they taking me?

Why are they all smiling?

Did something funny happen?

Why am I being expelled from mum's uterus?

Did I forget to pay rent?

Take me back

Nooo! Ah, milk...

yum!

hmmmm.... I could get used to this new place...

Tiffany Rehbein

Cheyenne, Wyoming, USA

Hour 19

The Milky Way

That night, I stood opposite of Cassiopeia
reading for her as she smiled, iciness
separating us. I floated from her
into outer space,
steam rising.

Orion hovered, casting a shadow
over her, eyes locking with mine.
Instead, I sipped from the Big Dipper,
spent 84 years traveling with Uranus.
I dated Aquarius,
befriended Ursa Minor,
that lovable bear,
surfed on the rings of Jupiter,
laughing without a sound. I danced a slow dance
with each of Saturn's moons, taking a bow after the ninth
set me free. My muted mouth moving, wordless.

The Queen gazed in the mirror

as I back floated through the Milky Way.

Ramona Elke

Mission, British Columbia, Canada

Hour 23

the return of the sun

my beach blanket smells of lake plants and sun.
I never knew I had a beach blanket
in these years of body shame
and black and white images
from a life I did not want photographed.

now I live in colour
and the whole world smells like sunshine dried clothing
and tastes like orange freezies
and sangria.

or the seductive taste of sweet strawberries
or watermelon;
the juices of both,
or either,
running down my chin in dribbles,
reminding me of you
and your sweetness.

Now I live in colour

and all I want is to feel the sun on my skin

and smell the heat of the day near water,

fill my head with reggae,

and read a library of books

from the warm sands of some local beach.

I want to live Baudelaire by sunset,

whispering his words,

French and all,

to the swooping bats

or

to a beautiful, receptive lover

who will then take me in his arms

and mouth

and love me to collapse under the Milky Way –

our naked, blessed bodies

glistening by starlight to show us what we are truly made of.

Now that I feel alive and loved,

I need to taste the sun so often it burns my tongue

so that my words are fire when I speak them

or your mouth ignites when I kiss you

or you burst into flames when I take you in my mouth.

I have walked too oft in the shadows these past years,
now it is time to walk in the sun.

Kiba Elunal

Tomball, Texas, USA

The Archer

There's no greater feeling than that of life traveling through you.
The creaking of the wood,

the stretch of the string.

With my feet firmly planted and head pointed towards my
target,

in that moment, I can feel the very earth turning beneath me.

My ancestors whisper their secrets in my ears, and the scent of
life flows through me.

I take a deep breath, trying to savor the sensation of the world's
soul as it fills my entire body.

My fingers uncurl. It's not a loss of control, but a willing
surrender to the elements of nature.

The string, once restrained, snaps to. The souls leave me in a
sudden rush of wind.

Donna Meyer
West Virginia, USA
Hour 3

hanging the lights

shivering in the snow
I hold one end
of a long string of
multi-colored lights
a queue of gems
that stretches
from my hand
to my brother
high on the ladder

the cold doesn't
seem to bother him
nor the height
nor the precariousness
as he reaches out
along the eves
and hooks the lights
on timeworn nails

he likes the doing of it
but seems not to care
for the result.
I like the effect
of the house lit up,
so cheery
on a cold winter's night
I want only to skip ahead
to the full effect

together,
the laborer
and the poet,
we construct
this portrait of Christmas

Aditi Mahajan
India
Hour 12

Mother Tongue

I never forgot this language—
the way my tongue should roll
to pronounce the words

The pen doesn't fumble
when I try to form curves
of the alphabets

The words are
the warm blanket
in the frost

The prose is
the lost home
which I found too late

The songs
have a tune which
resonates with my breath

I had left my mother tongue

but its existence

never ceased within me

Roy Mark Azanza Corrales

Quezon City, Philippines

Appreciating the Colors of the World

Waking up in the world full of colors and hues

Color schema in learning the walks of life

Artful crafts illuminating the simple clues

Nothing surely can lead to strife

Verbatim the knowledge

Marking in its steps of combination

Working like steps as to ledge

Coloring the blank space a notion

Speck and span in our world illuminates

Every shade of gray, colorful hues of red and orange

Traversing times arriving in its palettes animates

Always cascading in all ranges

Moving much in the colors of realm deriving

World of life and love illuminating surely arriving

Maritza Martínez Mejía

Miami, Florida, USA

Homeless

Walking the streets day and night

begging for food

searching for job

looking for shelter

I found

some leftovers

no opportunities

close doors

I wondered

Who am I?

Where is my place?

to sleep tonight!

Joyce L. Bugbee

Higganum, Connecticut, USA

Hour 13

Connections

a phone

a camera

a clock

a notepad

voicemail

text alert

news and weather

traffic report

entertainment

one device

does it all

and more

I'm sure

Teri Harroun
Longmont, Colorado, USA
Hour 15

Untitled

it is not a sin to wear pants:

Mulan, St. Joan of Arc, Marinus, Pope Joan, Anne Bonny
it is not a sin to wear pants

to disguise yourself
as a man
to do the things
peculiarly
reserved for men,
it is not a sin to wear pants

to be pirate or priest
or military might
to study in university
to travel in safety
or farm on your own,
it is not a sin to wear pants

be subversive, oh, be subversive
claim what is yours
live what you dream

pave way for the next generation

or mine,

it is not a sin to wear pants

one day little girls

will be inspired by you

your courage

your creativity

your persistence,

and they will wear pants

but not in disguise,

it is not a sin to wear pants

Steve Kalinowski
Tucson, Arizona, USA

Tremors

The Earth Mother has been with child,
and the child has mother much beguiled.

The child he kicks then kicks some more.
His mother shakes down to her core.

The humans know for when he kicks.
The Earth, it quakes and breaks their bricks.

Yes Ruau-Moko is never calm,
and Papa can't escape not even in Guam.

So the next time you feel the Earth quake
it is just Ruau-Moko making Papa shake.

Kaye Vivian
Houston, Texas, USA
Hour 16

Maid Marian's Lament

Oh, for a jug and my Robin beside.
Astride his horse, together we'd ride
Along the fair road to the village of Quay
And we'd sing jolly-lolly-o-lay, o-lay,
We'd sing jolly-lolly-o-lay.

He left me to fade in this castle so grey
With the nuns and the friars and his battle dray,
Keepin' his sword for the next fightin' day,
Why sing jolly-lolly-o-lay, o-lay?
Can't sing jolly-lolly-o-lay.

Our Little John came to see me this morn,
He spoke of the green men and left me his horn,
Sayin' "Use this to call me at evenin' or morn,
And I'll come," jolly-lolly-o-lay, o-lay,
I'll come. jolly-lolly-o-lay.

I know in my heart that day will not come.

My Robin is gone, and I soon will be done,

The love of a man will not bring us to one,

So I sing jolly-lolly-o-lay, o-lay,

And mourn jolly-lolly-o-lay.

(slowly)

The Sheriff of Nottingham sent us his men,

To carry me off hoping I'd marry him.

He'll find but a cold corpse and well-poisoned rim,

And no lady to sing jolly-lolly-o-lay,

She is gone jolly-lolly-o-lay.

Gina Surgeon

Atlanta, Georgia, USA

Hour 17

Aging

Would someone please help me find my keys?

I've looked in the living room, dining room, and on the kitchen sink.

I have checked the bedroom, refrigerator, everywhere that I could think.

Asked the dog, his head said, "no"

Asked the cat and, well, you know

I am late and I've lost them once again

Wait! They are right here in my hand.

Janus Joy Miller,
Escondido, California, USA

Lesson in Gardening

My yellow squash died.
Three of them I drenched
until the cool of spring
rotted their roots.
I watered and they did not grow,
and so, I watered more
and more, for hours at a time
each and every morn.
Behind them, the zucchini went.
And, oh! The butternut, too!
My thumb now brown as matter spent
because I water too soon.

Evangeline C. Cube
Quezon City, Metro Manila, Philippines
Hour 13

At a Loss

Staring at nothing, lost in her world
Misty-eyed, glazy
Indefatigable sorrow, unrelenting, deafening
Silent sobbing
The eyes, the eyes, says it all

Will there be no let-up?
Will it be a continuing restlessness?
It was half-expected, the excruciating pain,
Yet still, she's hurting

Unsuspectingly the torrential tears, non-stop
Welcome or not, it's the relief that's due her
The outpourings of hurts, pains, aches
The free-flowing saline fluid, unburdening
Loosening up the heaviness inside

At that, the dam abated
Just like when it started, unceremoniously

And with it, de-constriction

A hiatus, albeit temporary

A relief, a great sign of relief...

Until the next onslaught...

Nonet

you open your eyes and look at me

lashes fluttering, seduction

a whip threatening to strike

Venus' antagonist

a slash across the

immobile face

erotic

hatred

dealt

Phillip T. Stephens
Austin, Texas, USA
Hour 24

Beach Bathing on Sunday Afternoons

From space
the umbrellas that
shade the swimmers
look like pollen.
Row after row
following the shore
like a pollen garden
precisely planned.
Like an obsession:
this grid yellow,
this grid blue,
each grain waiting
for wind or wings of
butterflies to
bear them away.
Sometimes
I wonder if the
world will sneeze,
clear the infection.
Start something new.

Danielle Martin
Trinidad and Tobago
Hour 1

Do you hear me?

I hear the sounds between raindrops
the words you do not say, the thoughts you drop my way
But do you hear me?
The answers tucked away in warm blankets of sarcasm
the laughter that rings out to hide my fear
a subtle pause placed here and there

My silence, do you hear?

Danielle Wong
Montreal, Quebec, Canada
Hour 23

Mom

Her gnarled knuckles
knitted sweaters and blankets
faster and more tenderly
than any machine.

These same knuckles
kneaded the earth around the fruit,
around the vegetables
she tended daily.

These strong knuckles
kneaded pastry and cookie
dough and bread gingerly,
filling the air

with her perfume
concocted from aromas
of oatmeal, tortière, and creton;
hours spent by the stove.

And when I put on
new clothes, I wait for the scrape
of forlorn pins hiding,
her eyes smiling

with a straight face,
biting her lips and holding
back laughter at how she forgot
again and says,

"Oopsalie".

A Stone Path

a stone path

shining with fallen leaves

leads to a peaceful

lake in forgotten woods

the home to my verses

Soft Voice

My heart just melted.
With your soft voice.

You turn my heart.
 Into love

Final Trip to Allahabad

that was our final trip together,

the Maha Kumbh Mela in Allahabad

where you asked me to donate clothes to a Sanyasin;

I did, but the loin cloth that I wore,

you smiled, assuring me

and the Sanyasin vanished in the crowd;

half of your soul vanished too…

people praised me,

"To bring mother for pilgrimage is

washing away your sins," they said.

you smiled, assuring me again…

time has flown mother;

I still miss your assuring smile

and your soul that vanished too…

Deborah Dalton
Charlotte, North Carolina, USA
Hour 7

Wisdom Invites Madness

(Ecclesiastes 2:1-11)

Examine my heart

      it beats

      intricate melodies

      intoxicating

      on repeat

Examine my thoughts

      inspiration

      tracing genius

      plotting against

      defeat

Examine my hands

open for giving
gripped for living
raised for what
my religion holds

Examine my motives

pulls to lofty goals
leading to darkness
buried beneath layers
of unquenchable soil

Examine my prayers

pleadings and
praisings and
prying away with intercession
seeking limitless grace
unwarranted favor

Examine my love
balanced under the
threshold of unconditional
two-steps behind
what is pure and perpetual

Examine my feet

        scaling mountains

        climbing down stairs

        running empty races

        walking in despair

Examine my existence

        a philosophical

        conundrum

        questioning if I am really

        and truly

        here

Amanda Potter
Jacksonville, Florida, USA
Hour 21

Exhausted Exhilaration

Body tired
    brain stone cold

Wired

Here we are
    longing, dreading

Finish line in sight
    three more to go

High on caffeine
    and inspiration

Music blasting, silently
    exhausting, batteries

Running on empty
    living like renegades

Love the underdogs

Parade! Parade!
Did the circus come to town?

We are, the Poets of the night

It's always different
then when it came before

Exaggeration?
That's what words are for!

Shirley Durr
Minneapolis, Minnesota, USA
Hour 23

Anticipating Betrayal

With my sister, I anticipated betrayal.
She never was what she said

When we were young, she was god.
I adored her,
worshiped her,
feared her,
and yearned to be in her image

Every time I thought she would
be my savior
she left me bereft of hope
with broken covenant
and unfulfilled promises

I adored my sister for her strong persona
but never was able to fit myself in her image.
She burned hot and spontaneously
I simmered slowly,
duly deliberately.
She was quick to see an advantage

162

and take it.
I was the advantage she took.

Because she was god, her cruelest acts were proof
of her awesome power
her fearsome wrath
her benevolent generosity.

Even in my pain
which she caused
I thanked her for taking time for me.
Mostly, she forgot I existed.

Sometimes in the twilight gods fade into oblivion
But they do not die
Even her death betrayed me
For she left me incomplete

I think now that I betrayed her
With my adulation

If only I could bring her back
To replace my obsequious adoration
With love

J.L. Wright

Bellingham, Washington, USA

Hour 13

Early light in Poodledom

Each day I spend dawn waiting

clicker training they call it.

Instead I am just anticipating.

I yawn and stretch they sit,

drink coffee in bed,

play games until they quit.

One asks if I've been fed

as the other presses a button

I dance before I am led

by a leash on my morning walk

C.R. Sierra
Derbyshire, UK
Hour 19

Cosmic Ruin

Cold

darkness

unending

pinpricks of light

beam across the black

streaking through dimensions

alien to human space

crossing barriers of physics

and entering the abstract realms of

fantasy and science fiction fables

unexplored corners of furthest time-space

await the arrival of matter

molecules to shape a new world

intelligence to force it

from chaos to order

speeding entropy

to stop its growth

an ending

frozen

Cold

Gleaning

Corn grew in the flowerpot
I wasn't the sower
I would not allow inhabitation

but...

I acquiesced to her mission,
she might want to observe,
anticipate her crop's abundance

Tall and slender it stretched
among bushy bloomed stems
of vibrant garnet and magentas

Tucked between mints
it widened as required

Under rain it withstood,
in wind bend it held

We waited, squirrel and I,
not giving directions,
only room for its reach
and a bit of top dressing

and I wonder...

If I were to start over
where would I choose to sow,
would my gardener be tender
to my waxing

Cafe Writer

Words slipping free of my pens.
Stories unfolding from depths of thoughts.
Stretching to fill the page.

But my stories are left half done.
Pen unsure of what is coming next.
All action gone to calm quiet.
The hero losing the need to save.
Story frozen and left in a file.

My eyes glance around the cafe.
Everyone living a story.
Maybe some writing new ones too.
Some also only getting half down.
Not able to finish the story.
Maybe the end is too sad.
Or it became too cliché.
Or maybe I am the only one lost.

Reminiscence

The boxes I put myself in are getting smaller.

As a child of seven summers,
when my bare feet knew the grasses well,
I was Odysseus at Troy,
carving a way through the enemy rhododendrons.

I spoke at the midnight hour on August fifteen,
I was fifteen then,
my voice rose high and clear,
my dreams torched the sky.

I loved this girl from the next neighborhood,
pretty in peony pink hijab,
the youth did not know when to back down,
the youth did not know how not to love.

Now that the girl is gone,
the dreams have withered away;

and the child gave way a long ago

to the husk of a man that I have become.

K.C. Wolfe

Los Angeles, California, USA

Hour 2

Brush Strokes

How to say how I long for you

An obsession, black, oozing,

Gripping my mind with inky talons

I'll handle it (with my hands) I'll handle it.

Gripping. My fingers lock around its neck and I squeeze.

I'll squeeze until it bursts in colors of crimson and ultramarine,

Black and white and emerald green. Yellow oxide. Colors of

flames and explosions. Colors of forests

and dark haunted lakes. Sunsets, fogged banks, and cityscapes

I'll squeeze these tubes of color onto a palette and load them

onto bristles, real and synthetic.

The only way to tell you what it is you do to me

Is through shades of acrylic. Blended on stretched canvas.

Deanna Ngai

Calgary, Alberta, Canada

Hour 14

The Fruits of my Labor

I stand at the open window
    on an evening warm and damp.
The steam rises off the canning pot
    I slowly switch on a lamp.
The tomatoes in their canning jars,
    the children at my elbow.
At the open window I stand,
    hear the frogs croak their nightly show.
One great mystery in life
    is how I came to be,
standing in my raincoat
    with a sea of children surrounding me.

Jeannine Kauffmann

Worthing, UK

Hour 12

Pancakes are Round

Pancakes are round.

they smell of childhood forgotten memories,

they bring with them a huge sadness,

of children who have left the hearth.

They are

warm, yellow and crispy

the way I like them

but they make me feel lonely,

isolate,

as an adult,

they are Robinson Crusoe food,

marooned on a deserted island.

Did he miss pancakes?

He could have some of mine,

Jam and then some with cheese,

and maybe some for tomorrow's breakfast,

used to freeze some for a quick snack for the children.

Pancakes are round or ought to be

but they give nostalgia a new meaning.

David L. Wilson
Kihei, Hawaii, USA
Hour 18

At the Circus

It was a public hallway

at the Westchester County Center

surrounding the arena

hosting the circus

Must have been intermission

for the boy to be there

and see

a clown in full make-up and outfit smoking

into the pay phone

and hear the voice

of an everyday adult

arguing about money

the elastic holding his strawberry nose in place

plainly visible

Seeing an eagle, close up

My first trip to Kolkata, after a decade,
with my family, meant visiting all the
important tourist spots. One such activity

was the ferry ride on river Hooghly, against
the backdrop of Howrah Bridge. As we waited
for our ferry, enjoying the river's flow,

and cool, gentle breeze against our skin,
my son tugged on my arms and drew my attention
towards a gigantic eagle perched on the plank,

a few feet away from where we stood. With fierce,
glittering eyes, its brown wings merging with
the color of floorboard leading to the ferry

point, the eagle was a sight to behold. We took
a few steps back and slowly switched on our phones,
watching out for the eagle's discomfort. We clicked

a few pictures as it stared at us, unblinking.
The ferry honked as it came closer. We kept looking
at the eagle and it continued to watch us, as we stepped

into the ferry. It spread its magnificent wings, shook
its head and soared into the sky. We continued watching
it, till we could see it no more and then enjoyed our ride.

Missouri Blues

It will be 2045 before a solar eclipse comes to me
when I am eighty-four.
The closest place I can see it now
is Liberty, Missouri.

Five and a half hours straight north.

Missouri has just been put on high travel alert
by the NAACP and the Missouri ACLU.
Tell me, if I follow the North Star to see the sun
will I be able to navigate back home to you?

Sreelatha Chakravarty
Mumbai, India
Hour 18

Table for two, please...

Can we have
a table for two,
waiter?
It is so full…

Yes, sir, it is;
it is monsoon
and none will take
the outdoors and the wind.

Oh, then let's brave, dear,
the outdoorsy;
under the umbrella
with blue-yellow stripes, hurry,
let's go sit
and create a few memories;

Why not, darling
the chairs are so antique,

almost rustic;

the food here is always the same,

watered down spices; butter-greased;

but, at least, the drinks may taste

heady with elixir of heavens mixed.

Right, madam,

you'll both be in good company

of each other;

we always have table for two arranged,

for a couple that were brought together,

for such fine dining and wining,

in plump humor and exquisite taste.

T. Haven Morse
Evergreen, Texas, USA
Hour 12

Acrostic Writing

When I'm writing, I get lost in myself, lost in the moment,
lost in the story, lost in passionate imagination.

Right-hand controls the wielded weapon, while the left
hangs on for dear life, keeping sanity intact for us all.

Infinite are the possible stories, characters, settings, and
images, to set them all free at once, is how I fill my pages.

Tender are the moments when a protagonist dies or
the heroine meets the man of her dreams, during his birth.

Infectious is the drug of spirited discovery, when the muse
plays her music in my mind, and I dance to the rhythm.

Never can I go back from this life I've established, created,
molded, and now relish more than I ever thought I would.

Grateful is the emotion that springs forth every day that I
wake up to a blank page and declare, "I am a writer."

Shobha Elizabeth John

Kerala, India

Hour 21

Neo-colonized Me

Lazing around on my retro couch

I shake my head and sigh

As the news channel stumps me

With its tirade on loss of culture

While I twirl a pen with a label

Which says it is made in China

And my mind wanders through nations

And notions and talks about nationality

But I stop as I realize

I'm not too sure where I belong, mentally

I stand with one foot firmly in the East

Another, dangling in the West

But that does not even make any sense

Perpetual confusion abounds in the voices

Of people like me who seem to be tainted

With a splash of multiple colours

'cause of some colonizing exploits by men of old

From before the time when I was born

And now with the internet, it's a small world after-all.

I who major in English Literature

But teach my niece my mother tongue

Listen to a German composer's music

While studying about the French Revolution

Wears my Indian traditional outfit to a party

Where my friend hums a Spanish song

And talks about studying abroad.

I, whose childhood was carved

Out of Grimm's Fairy Tales and Blyton's 'Famous Five'

Reads works of Nigerian authors more

Than that of my neighbour who writes.

My brother roots for Barcelona and shouts at the TV at 3 am

I who crave Mexican food and ends up eating pizza

Calls my aunt in Australia to ask her about the weather

Discusses American Politics sipping latte

With a Professor of Sanskrit at the University of Stockholm.

The whole world is on my bucket list to visit

And I'll be going some day I say

But I forgot where I was going with this

Except to ask, can someone help me out

Give my confused thoughts a break

Place this neo-colonized me

(not too sure what that means)

Somewhere on the 2-D map of the world
I hold in my hand.

Elizabeth Durusau

Athens, Georgia, USA

Without a Mark

There are ways to kill without leaving a mark

Injuries to the heart

Blows to the soul

There is no exact science to this

One never knows how many hits it takes

Sometimes the system is weak but requires multiple strikes

Or the system is strong and yet only one blow will fell it

There is no exact science

There is no list of rules

And no one knows

When the last blow is dealt

But when the person falls

We all feel it

Evening Fog

October is the month the mists draw in.

These calm and freshly silent mornings now settle summer

and draw reluctant autumn to our door.

The evening fog falls low on crop-shorn fields

as rolls of rich, undulating white seep through the emptying

hedges

and fall in ragged scraps of soft, pale mist

that scatter loosely at our feet like something worn.

The animals will walk within this now – a second skin –

shielding themselves from hunter and from prey

while we, preparing for the still, small death of winter's blast

mourn what is concealed –

soon to be lost.

The Portrait

I stand alone, in an empty room
my gaze missing, my hunger hidden
he paints my curves with delicate lines
my nose, demanding attention.

The fabric dark and wanting against
my pale skin, waiting to be touched
by the maid as she peels from me
this velvet concoction.

This portrait for the wall, will watch
As l grow, tainted into my future.

Baby

wet from birth~

i gave you breath...

your spirit burns so bright!

how can I ever bury you?

Secrets

Secret lies that's what he told me
some tarty moments he was very shady
trust he would open up to me one day
this he never did.

Let the love flow no matter
where you go for my love
for you will never die
you have a piece of my heart
so use it wisely.

Let me dream of you all weekend
why don't you do the same
every moment away from you is like
a month or two daunting in the blues.

The Master and the Maid

Still she stood as the master ordered,

her maid's overalls were exchanged for a black revealing gown,

bought from the Maiden Fair store.

Her master was an artist,

everyone knew him,

she was privileged to work for him they said.

She wondered what the privilege was,

to stand for hours in a dress she was coerced to wear,

first with bribes, then threats.

She succumbed; she had brothers and sisters to feed.

She stood with rage running through her veins,

'Be still, don't shake', he said.

She stood still, planning in her head,

on how to purchase

the powder they said that can't be detected,

when given in small amounts over a long period of time.

A tiny smile appeared on her face,

he captured it succinctly though not knowing why.

Shrikaanth Krishnamurthy
Birmingham, UK
Hour 12

Alphabet Soup

what would I do

with a hundred words?

write you a letter?

a song in praise of you?

the beginning

of an epic?

an essay on beauty

pegged

to your gold standard?

if worth

were to be weighed

by quantity

and adherence to rules

surely this

would win a prize

fifty words

I have already reached

and so far

said nothing more

than when

I started this poem

and repetitions

do not count either

now I am sure

your are as befuddled

as I am

but if I were

to paraphrase all this

it would all

be said with my eyes

Sarah Johnson
New Jersey, USA
Hour 12

Wordstalk

I tossed and turned, as poets do,
With snips of words and poet's glue,
In hopes of making old sound new,
Before the Sandman came.

I won the bout, then drifted off
To dream of a Cecropia moth,
Until morning landed soft
In pitter-patter rain.

And laying there, I could not find,
Through thorough searching of my mind,
The words I'd won. Not one small sign.
No crumb or minute grain.

Thus, I am here again to wrest
And stalk the words my utmost best,
And catch them sleeping in their nest –
Before they fly again!

Kerry Kelly
Mayo, Ireland
Hour 24

Multiverse Haiku

Multiverses, one
Entangled in great nature
Complex creation

Vincent Leleux
London, UK
Hour 22

Money Note Poet

To write his love journal
and his poems
he uses banknotes

To write short poems
he takes 1 dollar notes
for the longest
the 100 money notes

And sell them 10 times
what their value says
Most of his words
are not readable
on the notes

But he's become
famous for doing this
and everybody got
his own work of art

Piece of poetry
on a banknote
because over time
they are worth
even much more

He got arrested
at the beginning
because it's illegal
to use money notes
to divert its use

That very story
made him famous
then everybody
started buying
his money note poems

He made quickly
a lot of money
so he was then allowed
to do it, and since then
has been on all TV shows

And everybody got his
money note poem
proudly hanging
on the wall of
their room or kitchen

Some even pray
make some altars
to worship the genius
of money note poem

Money Note Poet
is his name

Angel Rosen
Pittsburgh, Pennsylvania, USA
Hour 23

sleep tempest

In all of this, I may
have been the thunderstorm
and the best part of the rain.
The gentle roars,
the ballet of droplets,
the dim porch lights,
a cool flicker,
the strip-tease of lightning,
the sleep weather,
the gray.

Mel Neet

Kansas City, Missouri, USA

Hour 14

What I've Got

It's evening
and, finally, I've got my market tomatoes and holy basil.

More adults than children crowded the lines, but, in my raincoat,
I'm impervious.
With no rancor, I manage to elbow through the throngs.

I've funds enough for what I need
and almost feel I've been peculating
when I look inside my bag.

Overhead, the rain of frogs
and lizards begins just as I
catch one of the streetcars

that are like jars of cool air
from the steam of the sidewalks.
Waiting, still, are more shoppers

for whom the city is a mystery.

Dinner Date

At a table for two
we sat and smiled
as couples do on a date
early in a budding relationship.

That night marked a demarcation in our lives.

She flashed her radiant smile,
her delicate perfect features
framed with angelic curls,
a crystal on a chain around her neck,
her peasant blouse showing off her good shoulders.

From that night came a new career, parenthood, stability,
instability, and sadness.

I was in a brilliant, happy phase,
full of vitality and creativity
fairly wise and not too arrogant,

with hair still framing my rugged features,
contact lenses letting my soft eyes show.

The biological clock was ticking for both of us.
This was my callback audition for sperm donor, parent, partner,
life mate, lover.

I never believed this spectacular creature
could really want humongous bumbling me.
I drove her crazy with my insecurity,
but eventually she convinced me she loved me.
I adored her so much I was afraid to show it,
hiding behind a bit of gruffness.

That night was the beginning of two wonderful children, ten
eventful years together,
the golden time that divided my long youth from my elderly
disabled days.

I don't remember anything that happened that night
at that table for two,
just an indelible picture of two people joining their lives,
blessed by the soft lights of a nice restaurant

on a momentous dinner date.

Eternally Trapped

There she lay,
still today;
Trapped inside a body,
in a bay.

They bury her there,
hoping no one would say,
'who is that girl in the bay?'

There was no girl,
no girl in that bay.
Only a demon that lay,
lay asleep.
Waiting for her prey.

She preys on the weak.
She preys on the caring.

So, if you see her be sure,

be sure to leave her laying.

Laying in the dirty swamp,

where demons like her belong.

Comfort

Seeing my bold child,

Taking off her training wheels,

Oddly reassures.

Seema Kapur
Arizona, USA
Hour 19

Circle of poetry

Early finishers
late starters
each will find
radiant day
in the space
we all are floating
waiting a place
to sit and watch the space
view from below is distorted

Without space....
the stars would have
nowhere to shine,
the earth and the moon would
no longer dance
the sky would no longer hold
the clouds in its embrace
and you would have
no room to move

What magic is in the space

its landscape is huge

far more than we all can fill

we all are like

overlapping petals

of different flowers;

spreading energy

reaching everyone

across vast space;

caressing and strengthening

our resolve

and complete

our circle of poetry!

Kaili Kinnon
Toronto, Ontario, Canada
Hour 6

The Colour blue

Deep gladness, great hunger –
having wondered if I would ever get beyond,
I wonder no more.

The green is lavish, perfect –
I'm enamoured of each stretching pine,
I wonder no more.

I inherited black clothes, the colour blue –
embracing them as my mother before me,
I wonder no more.

Aliice Black

Los Angeles, California, USA

Hour 15

Goddess

sweet Gaia

rustling through effervescent decades

she is the spiraling serpent that plucked the apple from the tree

she is the root of the tree.

she is Persephone

licking pomegranate seeds, her fruit of the dead.

she is unafraid of the dead, unafraid of the underworld.

she is what made Orpheus look back.

it was she

that drew iron tears down Pluto's cheek.

and then reborn as

Venus spawning from the sea.

she is in the waves of every mouth

a God has ever kissed.

she is in the frail wrist of the fading,

wading in the tides of dried flowers

and humble offerings.

what of Psyche?

what of the personification of soul?

wraps you up in satin sheets

and eats you whole.

pours into every vein

vain like Narcissus,

held in every echo.

just like Echo, speaking only mirrors of her love.

Gaia, my love.

pull you into the river to quiver along the valleys,

gripping talons into the earth.

she is rebirth.

infinite.

Eternity Now

You can put it up in neon
or carry it on a sign,
just as long as people know,
the end is nigh.
It governed your vote for president,
how much you long for His return.
It's had something to do with everything,
from who you married to the way you spurn
your gay relative, and how you discern
what to like on Facebook, and what to turn
away. I must admit I'm winging it, on Judgement Day.

Simona Frosin

Romania

Hour 1

The Four Elements

Concert on the beach,

passion is rekindled,

the fire inside is growing,

lucky to have the sea nearby.

Pigeons are crossing the sky,

defying the hot sand under our feet.

Why don't we also have wings?

I bet that we would use them better than Icarus!

Tracy Elizabeth Plath
El Paso, Texas, USA
Hour 15

Metamorphosis

I drove alone to the desert at solstice
one cold and moonlit December night
to test the theory of animals
that spoke human tongues at midnight
and ask them of wooden longboats
and round shields, buried in southwest sands.

My whimsy returned me to far older wisdom,
plunged into a deeper past,
a Viking legacy whose genetic remainder
in me until now was ice-water eyes, ashen hair,
and a thirsting desire in this new world desert
to know just what lay over the horizon.

The flickering flames warmed my body at fireside
and freed my mind to wander through
mysterious sounds that layered the still night:
crackling and popping mesquite, *screeing*

crickets, and the shivering ululation of a single
coyote's cry to the waxing moon.

The night deepened, approached zenith,
and moonlight and wood-smoke coalesced
in front of my stunned eyes into a long snout,
gleaming teeth, and golden eyes. A throaty voice
emerged as if from the very night:
Welcome, Coyote grunted,

You've taken so long to return, Loki.
A long, pink tongue swiped my cheek,
a coyote's kiss, and I howled an irresistible
duet with my trickster brother, Coyote,
in furred glory
to the engorged and brilliant moon.

Snigdha Shaw
Kolkata, India
Hour 24

Window

The windows of my heart,

that peeps into reality,

effacing off the mud,

got stuck with time.

The window to my longing desire,

to jump and dance,

seeing the birds chirping,

and dirty glance of the rainbow.

The window of my yearning love,

waiting for the day to come.

To be loved,

the way these,

love birds show their prance.

Angela Feathers
Charleston, South Carolina, USA
Hour 19

Ball Lightning

When my voice is old,
I'd like to sing into a gorge,
into the Marianas Trench.
I want my brow to grow heavy,
bearing peaches, to feel
the weight of decades on
my hips, to own a splintered
fractal of human history.
When my hair is white and
silver, I'll unleash the stars
of my braid, arthritic
opening to God. My hunched
spine will crack open, wrinkled
skin peeling away, bone
popping and curling until
the husk of
Who I Thought I Was
falls away, blows away, to
reveal the ball of light inside.

Reunion

The first thing she asks
after inquiring about me, while
gripping me in enveloping hug:
how my wife is, the kids are
we talk amiably, deeply
about our lives, families. Stuff.
I see in her eyes what I have
since junior high; this she knows
her impossible-to-dislike
husband greets me warmly, joins
us in conversation, laughter
their body language, comfortable
any awkwardness that did exist
no longer does, though he knows
that I understand, better than most
what has always been in her eyes
it takes more self-control than I
think I have, to not say aloud, in

reckless triumph, "But I loved her
twenty years before you showed up"
knowing nothing is to be gained
playing 'nan-nah-nan-nah, boo-boo'
with the beautiful muse who never
loved me then, but oddly, does now.

Laurie McKay
Cadillac, Michigan, USA
Hour 7

Baby Girl

My baby girl, full of Grace
strong, beautiful, radiant.
Seeing past the pain
until
it overwhelms and engulfs once more.

My baby girl, full of Grace,
trying to breathe
trying to calm
until
she can rest, but not progress.

My baby girl, full of Grace
trying so hard,
over time and pain
until
there is progress with no results

My baby girl, full of Grace
given an emotional decision

without food or sleep

until

she chooses the necessary, but not emergency

My baby girl, full of Grace,

until

her baby, beautiful Grace

open eyed, ready to be

In her arms and heart.

Window

My alarm clock buzzing and telling me to wake up from a short nap and so my brain asked me, to check the next prompt for 23 hours poetry marathon.

And this bright and glaring sun rays penetrate through the bedroom window's curtain and greeting me to a blessed morning.

The sun warm touch, gave me the energy to continue my 24 hours journey.

I could hear birds chirping and cheer me to reach the finish line of the marathon.

it was a marvelous day, when I looked out of the window, to see people up on their feet and ready for a brand new day.

Some were going to the park for an early morning walk and some to their church of worship.

Upon my waking up, it was like,

As if, I got 8 hours of deep sleep, instead of 20 minutes break from writing poems.

I was already up before the clock warn me. I made a cup of coffee and open the window to feel the cool breeze and

Instead, I got a sun kiss from Mr. Sun.

Life's Unpredictable Itinerary

Yesterday, I liked my high school love.

Today, I love my husband that was sent from above.

Yesterday, I thought our love had fallen apart.

Today, I know that together we will make it through.

Yesterday, I frowned at the thought of having too many kids.

Today, I smile because my heart is filled with joy as I learned
that we could have many more.

Yesterday, I doubted I would ever be free to write just one
poem.

Today, I believe I can write as many that will come.

Yesterday, I wished my life would be easier.

Today, I pray and many doors came open.

Aaron Conklin
Warrensburg, Missouri, USA
Hour 3

Dancing Shadow

The silhouette of my soul is a dancing shadow,
a bestial revelry in the last hours of day,
I beckon the advancing throat of night.

I celebrate the freedom of my spirit
with swaying arms that could embrace the entire horizon.
I expel the filing system of tail lights retreating,
as a marching pestilence receding from my being,
and shed the masked perspective of singularity.

I reject the notion of being made to feel small
and enlarge myself beyond what fixated fears will have me see.
I unleash the multitudes of my infinity
to serenade the rats with my seductive song
and welcome the hordes of the hopeless
to follow me to the end of the world.

Caitlin Thomson

Bellingham, Washington, USA

Hour 24

Chaos Loop Timed

This day a heady mess, the stairs are strewn
with feathered boas, books are stacked in unsteady
piles. This house and me, a veer toward madness,
I pile quilts till they are a bed, sleep

with feathered boas, books are stacked in unsteady
towers. Every day a different battle, but at night
I pile quilts till they are a bed, sleep,
forgetting all about my encounters with peacocks and

towers. Every day a different battle, but at night
there is sleep and dreams to help me
forget my encounters with peacocks and
saxophones, the professional tomato grower.

Now there is sleep and dreams to help me.
This day a heady mess, the stairs are strewn
with saxophones, tomatoes on their vines.
This house and me, a veer toward madness.

Disha Khanna
Phagwara, India
Hour 6

Words Can Do Wonders

Words have quality;
That is the reality.

Words can deceive;
Like water through a sieve.

Must be properly blended,
Words once apprehended.

Words once said,
Later we may dread.

The words need weighing ,
When you recite an old saying.

Words that generate heat,
Try not to repeat.

Words that are measured,

Forever will be treasured.

Words once uttered,
Later we may dread.

Heartfelt word,
Is better heard

Words that say nothing,
Can amount to something

Choose your words better,
If it is your last letter

With words you must play,
When you know what to say

Best words in their best disorder,
Will make room for fodder

Megan R Saturley

Austin, Texas, USA

His body moved with the wind

His body moved with the wind,

a tornado of some sort.

Running through the forest, mother nature's highest court.

Woodland creatures turn to glance, but he's far gone.

The course of his path is already drawn.

Leaves and flowers gust with his blast,

dodging obstacles and branches steadfast.

His feet splash in the water as he winds with the river.

He gasps hard for air, but his lungs won't deliver.

His legs start to spark as if striking flint.

Leaves scorch fast, his fire footprint.

Further and further he runs his path

leaving much debris in his aftermath.

He's choking for air, his lungs at their best,

ignoring fatigue, that foul pest.

But he doubts his body and what energy he has left

thinking of the course and its wide breadth.

He slows to a stop. The forest is dead.

He pauses, then pushes, because it's all in your head.

Missing

I don't want to write about the things I miss.
It will only make me miss them more.

The soft silky ears
of my faithful,
though misbehaved,
companion;

The squared off letters
on the top left corners
of envelopes that carried
short notes and news
and AAA memberships
from home;

The warmth of a body
wrapped around mine
as I drifted off to sleep
on a cold winter's night;

The paycheck I had
when I hated my job
but felt free to go
out to dinner;

My house in the woods
and the feeling I had
when I sat on the porch
with my big yellow dog
and my hot morning coffee;

The pain in my face
from smiling all day
as I drove wide-eyed
around the country;

The thrill that I felt
the first many times
people traded their money
for things I'd created;

Feeling I had plenty of time,
and all things were still possible.

Carolyn L. Robinson
Baltimore, Maryland, USA
Hour 13

my world without you

i try to imagine a world without sun
it is easier than you think
for that would be my world without you

nothing would grow lush green
only scales and prickly leaves would crunch beneath my feet

at daybreak there would be no dew on the grass
or strong stem to glisten in the morning light
only dry stalk that would bend sorrowfully toward earth
the way i sometimes find it difficult
to force a smile from my lips when you are away

there would be no striking aura in the day's sky
just steel gray clouds;
a dull blank slate would blanket over me
like my dreams when you are not dancing in them.

Anita K. Boyle
Bellingham, Washington, USA
Hour 6

A Lesson Learned

In the old church,
on the hard, dark pews,
it grew hot and hotter
through the stained glass.

My little jacket was deep blue
with four buttons and two
pockets, one without a single hole.
A collection of gum-wads
were stuck under the bench,
some stickier than others.
My chubby fingers soon smelled
lusciously of peppermint,
clove, and spearmint.

And then came the sin, of course.
Who could resist? That devil.
Little kids do things like this:

Chewing other people's gum
without remorse. Savoring the flavors.
The understanding that, yes, it's true
that gum keeps its flavor
when put on the bedpost overnight.
Even someone else's gum.

Rachel Marco-Havens
Woodstock, New York, USA
Hour 24

Miss You

the smile in your eyes
used
to
be
lighter

your humor something that suits you well

we laughed often

I keep trying to return to those places
just for reference

Cinthia Albers
Kihei, Hawaii, USA
Hour 23

Missing

About 4 hours ago
I started missing you
You seemed to desert me
My brain started working in mysterious ways
Not making proper connections
Not making perfect sense
I just knew you were gone

You snuck out the door
Didn't make a sound
Left, deserted me

I know I didn't entice you to stay
I didn't give you reasoning
I didn't feed you those psychological
questions you love so much
I let you leave
I didn't try to stop you

But you and me,

We are a team,

Often estranged I know

I admit it's me, not you

We need each other

My dear, wonderful sanity

Sweet overworked friend

I hope you return in the morning

We can make a fresh start of things

We can find a way through this together.

This is only one night, a temporary setback

Don't leave angry

Get a good night's sleep

In the morning you will see

Everything will be fine.

J. Ryne Danielson
Brevard, North Carolina, USA

Lunacy

I wander rabbit-haunted meadows

waiting for the tick-fat moonrise.

Dew-soaked shadows stretch

stealth and melancholy beneath an ancient oak.

I carve myself into the roots

and whisper: I'm not me. I'm not me.

Pamela Gerber
Surf City, California, USA
Hour 13

I believe in the mystery

I believe in the mystery

—of what the frog choir sings

as they vibrate sound oscillating
breath from lungs to vocal cords
in late summer evening light,
the throaty croaks in full sermon
at the pulpit of love

—of how a wrist to elbow

measures the length of your foot,
or fingertip to fingertip is my height,
and the width of your mouth
maps the distance of pupil to pupil

—of the steam rising from tomatoes

beans, grape, radicchio, cucumbers,

and basil after the mid-day heat-pour

or the churning earthworm writhing

to the sound of five beating hearts

—of the soulless men who'd peculate

our children's futures on a handshake,

rob their health for pocketed pennies

by those who love their babies too.

www.ingramcontent.com/pod-product-compliance
Lightning Source LLC
Chambersburg PA
CBHW031620040426

42452CB00007B/599